A Young Child's Garden
of Christian Virtues

A Young Child's Garden
of
Christian
Virtues

Imaginative Ways to Plant God's Word in Toddlers' Hearts

Susan Lawrence

CPH
SAINT LOUIS

Ben, David, and Teresa,
May you always love and serve our Lord.

Cover photography: Jon Feingersh/The Stock Market

Scripture quotations taken from the HOLY BIBLE, NEW INTERNATIONAL VERSION®. NIV®. Copyright © 1973, 1978, 1984 by International Bible Society. Used by permission of Zondervan Publishing House. All rights reserved.

Copyright © 1998 Concordia Publishing House
3558 S. Jefferson Avenue, St. Louis, MO 63118-3968
Manufactured in the United States of America

Library of Congress Cataloging-in-Publication Data

Lawrence, Susan, 1950-
    A young child's garden of Christian virtues / Susan Lawrence.
       p.   cm.
    ISBN 0-570-05314-5
    1. Christian ethics. 2. Christian education of children. 3. moral development. 4.   Family—Religious life. I. Title.
BJ1251.L33   1998
249—dc21
                                       97-31705
                                          AC

3 4 5 6 7 8 9 10 11   07 06 05 04 03 02 01 00 99 98

Contents

As You Begin

Children—our heritage from the Lord! How wonderful that God entrusts His priceless children to our care. Part of our care includes asking the Holy Spirit's guidance as we plant biblical truths in their hearts.

This book will help you as you sow the seed of God's Word in your young child's heart. God's Spirit will bless your sharing of His Word, strengthening your toddler's faith in Jesus as the Savior and best friend who gave His life for your child.

Each devotion begins with a short reading from God's Word—the seed. Although the verses are printed in this book, let your child see you reading them from the Bible.

Each Scripture reading is reinforced with a finger play, action poem, or poem—a planting time designed to help your child remember the scriptural truth. Repeat the planting time activity several times during the week—even once a day. Important concepts are treated several times throughout the book. Young children love repetition, and God's Spirit will work powerfully through your time together.

A harvest time activity will help apply the truth to your child's own life. There is no better way to spend time together than in activities that will help your child live out the truths found in God's Word.

A short, child-friendly prayer will close your devotion. Encourage your child to repeat the prayer or pray in his or her own words.

It is never too early to share God's Word with your child. The minutes you spend together will reap an eternal harvest. Bring your child to Jesus' feet and hear Him say, "Let the little children come to Me."

I Know Who I Am!

The Seed: How great is the love the Father has [given] us, that we should be called children of God! And that is what we are! *1 John 3:1*

Planting Time

> God's little child,
> > *Place hands on head.*
> That's who I am!
> > *Point to self.*
> He loves me so much—
> > *Cross hands over heart.*
> I belong to Him.
> > *Form cross with index fingers.*

Harvest Time: Help your child draw a simple picture of herself with markers or crayons. As you draw, discuss how wonderful it is that God has made you both His children.

My Prayer: Thank You, God, for loving me so much. Thank You that I am Your child. In Jesus' name. Amen.

A Cross Means Love

The Seed: For God so loved the world that He gave His one and only Son, that whoever believes in Him shall not perish but have eternal life. *John 3:16*

Planting Time

> God loves us so much
> > *Cross hands over heart.*
> He sent His Son
> > *Point straight ahead.*
> To die on the cross
> > *Form cross with index fingers.*
> For everyone.
> > *Spread arms wide.*
>
> Because we believe,
> > *Cross hands over heart.*
> Eternal life He gives.
> > *Cup hands as if receiving a gift.*
> Now and in heaven,
> > *Point up.*
> With Him we will live.
> > *Hug self.*

Harvest Time: Eternal life and dying on the cross are difficult concepts for young children to understand. Read a simple Bible storybook about Jesus' death and resurrection. Make or purchase a simple cross to place on your kitchen table. Say, "A cross reminds us that Jesus loves us." Look for crosses when you go to church.

My Prayer

Dear God, thank You for loving me so much that You sent Jesus to the cross to die for me. In His name. Amen.

God's Word Is True

The Seed: For the Word of the LORD is right and true. *Psalm 33:4*

Planting Time: *Let your child hold a Bible while you say the following poem.*

> This book is God's Word,
> Perfect and true.
> His teachings are written
> For me and for you.

Harvest Time: The Bible is God's Word. It is true. In it God tells us all that He has done for us and how we can share His love. Read several of your child's favorite stories from the Bible. Let your child see you reading your Bible often. Take your Bible and a children's Bible or Bible storybook to church with you each week.

My Prayer: Dear God, I am so glad that You gave us Your Word. I believe it! In Jesus' name. Amen.

I Can Talk to God

The Seed: Be … faithful in prayer. *Romans 12:12*

Planting Time

> At home, at church, at play,
> > *Count to three on fingers.*
> When I am anywhere,
> > *Spread arms wide.*
> I can talk to God—
> > *Point to lips.*
> That's prayer!
> > *Fold hands.*
>
> In the morning or at night,
> > *Stretch as if waking up, then rest cheek on hands.*
> If it rains or if it's fair,
> > *Wiggle fingers for rain, then hold arms in a circle for the sun.*
> I can talk to God—
> > *Point to lips.*
> That's prayer!
> > *Fold hands.*
>
> If I'm as happy as can be
> > *Smile.*
> Or as cross as a little bear,
> > *Frown.*
> I can talk to God—
> > *Point to lips.*
> That's prayer!
> > *Fold hands.*

Harvest Time: Prayer is talking to God. When we are around other people, we can fold our hands and close our eyes so nothing will bother us while we pray. But we don't need to do that. We can talk to God anytime, anywhere. Let your child pray with you at special times during the day—when you go somewhere in the car, when you play a favorite game, when you prepare to eat or sleep.

My Prayer: Dear God, I'm glad I can talk to You anytime, anywhere. In Jesus' name. Amen.

God Made a Great World

The Seed; In the beginning God created the heavens and the earth. *Genesis 1:1*

Planting Time

From the stars up above
Point up.
To the earth down below,
Pat the ground.
God made it all—
Spread arms wide.
I know, I know!
Clap hands.

From the great big tree
Stretch arms up for branches.
To the dandelion I blow,
Blow at index finger.
God made it all—
Spread arms wide.
I know, I know!
Clap hands.

From the bird flying high
Flap arms.
To the turtle so slow,
Point to feet and take tiny steps.
God made it all—
Spread arms wide.
I know, I know.
Clap hands.

Harvest Time: If possible, take a nature walk with your child and gather leaves, grass, pinecones, seedpods, feathers, flowers or weeds, bark, pebbles, etc. Keep the items in a box or glue them to cardboard or poster board. As your child handles these items, explain that God made these things for us to enjoy, and we can help Him care for His creation.

My Prayer: Thank You, God, for the beautiful world You made. I like *(ask your child to name items from God's creation)* best. Help me take care of Your wonderful world. In Jesus' name. Amen.

Growing in Love

The Seed: Be imitators of God ... as dearly loved children. *Ephesians 5:1*

Planting Time

> I am God's little child,
> > *Point to self.*
> I know this is so;
> > *Nod head yes.*
> God keeps me close to Him
> > *Hug self.*
> As every day I grow.
> > *Raise hands above head.*
>
> I can't see God to know
> > *Place hands over eyes.*
> What He wants me to do,
> > *Raise palms in a questioning gesture.*
> But I can read my Bible.
> > *Form open book with hands.*
> I know His Word is true.
> > *Nod head yes.*
>
> My Bible book will tell me
> > *Form open book with hands.*
> All I need to know
> > *Nod head yes.*
> About God's love in Jesus
> > *Cross hands over heart.*
> As every day I grow.
> > *Raise hands overhead.*

Harvest Time: Purchase or make a simple growth chart for your child. Measure your child's height and mark it on the chart with the date. Then read 1 John 4:8 to your child: "Whoever does not love does not know God, because God is love." Explain that as God helps your child grow tall and strong, He will also help his love for Jesus to grow.

My Prayer: Dear God, thank You for helping me to grow tall. Help me to grow in love too. In Jesus' name. Amen.

God's Love Never Goes Away

The Seed: [Nothing] in all creation will be able to separate us from the love of God that is in Christ Jesus our Lord. *Romans 8:39*

Planting Time

God's love is always with me;
Cross hands over heart.
He won't take it away.
Shake head no.
When I'm happy, when I'm sad,
Smile, then frown.
His love is here to stay.
Cross hands over heart.

Anyplace that I can go,
Walk in place.
His love is always there.
Cross hands over heart.
Close to home or far away,
Point straight ahead.
His love is everywhere.
Spread arms wide.

It doesn't matter where I go,
Shake head no.
He loves me still, you see.
Cross hands over heart.

Nothing in the whole wide world
Spread arms wide.
Separates God's love from me.
Hug self.

Harvest Time: Play a game of peekaboo or hide-and-seek with your child. Tell her that though you and she can be separated (as in the game), nothing will ever separate her from God's love.

My Prayer: God, thank You for Your love that is always with me, no matter what I do or where I go. In Jesus' name. Amen.

My Home

The Seed: We have … an eternal house in heaven.
2 Corinthians 5:1

Planting Time: *Build a house with blocks or Lego plastic building blocks as you say this poem together.*

> I may live in a big white house
> Or one that's made of brick.
> An adobe house could be my home
> With walls so cool and thick.
>
> A trailer with wheels may be my home
> Or an apartment way up high.
> I might live on a houseboat
> Or a farm with cows close by.
>
> It doesn't matter where I live
> Or if my house is old or new.
> God gives me everything I need—
> A home in heaven too.

Harvest Time: Help your child draw a picture of your house or cut pictures of houses from catalogs, magazines, or newspapers. Tell your child that one day you will have a beautiful home in heaven with Jesus.

My Prayer: God, thank You for my home. Thank You for promising me a home in heaven too. In Jesus' name. Amen.

Jesus Makes Things Right

The Seed: All have sinned and fall short of the glory of God. *Romans 3:23*

Planting Time: *Place six dominoes or boxes in a row. Tip one over as you read each "negative" action. Stand them upright again as you read the last stanza.*

> When I disobey my parents;
> When I argue; when I pout;
> When mom says, "Play quietly,"
> And I just have to shout;
>
> When I use words that are unkind
> Or get mad when I don't win;
> I'm doing things that are not good.
> God's Word calls them "sin."
>
> God sent His Son, Jesus,
> To live a perfect life
> And die for us upon a cross
> To make the bad things right.

Harvest Time: Talk together about some sins that you have committed and some things that your child has done wrong. Pray together, asking God to forgive you both. Then celebrate your forgiveness by doing something fun together. Use the words "I am sorry" and "I forgive you" often in your home.

My Prayer: God, I am sorry when I sin. Thank You for sending Jesus to help me. Amen.

I Obey My Parents

The Seed: Children, obey your parents in the Lord, for this is right. *Ephesians 6:1*

Planting Time

> I will obey my mom and dad
>> *Nod head yes.*
> 'Cause they know what's best for me.
>> *Point to self.*
> Obeying them will please God too.
>> *Nod head yes.*
> It's what He wants, you see.
>> *Hold hands out, palms up.*

Harvest Time: Discuss some of your household rules and explain why they are important. Be sure to "catch" your child being good. Thank him for listening and following your instructions, for cleaning up his toys, or for helping you.

My Prayer: Dear God, thank You for my mom and dad. Help me to obey them. In Jesus' name. Amen.

11

God Lives in Me

The Seed: Your body is a temple of the Holy Spirit.
1 Corinthians 6:19

Planting Time

> From the top of my head
> > *Place hands on head.*
> To the tip of my toes,
> > *Touch toes.*
> All of my fingers,
> > *Wiggle fingers.*
> My knees, and my nose—
> > *Touch knees and nose.*
>
> This is God's temple.
> > *Point to self.*
> His Spirit lives in me.
> > *Cross hands over heart.*
> Caring for my body
> > *Hug self.*
> Is a special job you see.
> > *Nod head yes.*
>
> I'll eat healthy foods—
> > *Rub tummy.*
> Try some that are new—
> > *Nod head yes.*
> Exercise every day,
> > *Run in place.*
> And sleep plenty too.
> > *Rest head on hands.*

Harvest Time: Plan some activities your child can do to take care of her body—eat a healthy snack, exercise together, take a special bubble bath, read a favorite Bible story before going to sleep.

My Prayer: Dear God, thank You for my wonderful body. Help me to take good care of it so it is a good temple for You. In Jesus' name. Amen.

Growing Fruit

The Seed: The fruit of the Spirit is love, joy, peace, patience, kindness, goodness, faithfulness, gentleness and self-control. *Galatians 5:22–23*

Planting Time: *As a snack, prepare a fruit your child enjoys. Eat it as you say this poem.*

> I want to be a fruit tree
> And grow the fruit from God.
> But I won't have bark and branches
> Or roots down in the sod.
>
> I'll be loving, kind, and good,
> And full of peace and joy;
> I'll be faithful, I'll be gentle
> With every girl and boy.
>
> I'll have self-control,
> And everyone will know,
> I have the Holy Spirit
> Who makes this good fruit grow.

Harvest Time: Stand a small branch in a ball of clay inside a flowerpot. Cut fruit shapes from construction paper. Label them with the fruit of the Spirit: love, joy, peace, patience, kindness, goodness, faithfulness, gentleness, self-control. When your child models one of these qualities, hang that fruit on the "tree" with a piece of yarn. Help your child to understand the meanings of the words and the fact that the Holy Spirit helps us share God's love. You might say, "Thank you for being kind and helping me fold the towels. God's love is growing in you."

My Prayer: God, thank You for helping Your Holy Spirit's fruit to grow in me. Help me share Your love with everyone around me. In Jesus' name. Amen.

God Keeps Me Safe

The Seed: I will lie down and sleep in peace, for You alone, O LORD, make me dwell in safety. *Psalm 4:8*

Planting Time

> I go to bed
> > *Stretch and yawn.*
> And sleep in peace.
> > *Rest head on hands.*
> Jesus keeps me safe.
> > *Hug self.*
>
> Tomorrow
> > *Stretch and yawn.*
> I will run and play.
> > *Run in place.*
> Jesus keeps me safe.
> > *Hug self.*

Harvest Time: Use fabric pens to write the Bible verse on a plain pillowcase. Let your child add some designs of his own. When it's time for bed, read the verse together and thank Jesus for keeping you safe while you sleep.

My Prayer: Thank You, Jesus, for keeping me safe while I am sleeping and while I am playing. Amen.

14

Good Job!

The Seed: Let another praise you, and not your own mouth. *Proverbs 27:2*

Planting Time

>I won't brag
>And talk about me.
>I'll share God's love
>And let others see.
>
>And if I see
>Someone else doing good,
>I'll tell them so,
>Just as I should.

Harvest Time: Demonstrate for your child what it means to brag. Then point out that, rather than bragging about how good we are, we thank Jesus for helping us share His love. Help your child think of a friend, relative, or teacher who has shared Jesus' love. Have your child dictate a thank-you note for that person, then decorate it and "sign" it.

My Prayer: Dear God, help me to see the loving things that others do and thank them for those things. In Jesus' name. Amen.

Giving Thanks

The Seed: Give thanks to the LORD, for He is good.
Psalm 107:1

Planting Time

> I say thank You to God
>> *Fold hands.*
> For the good things He has done—
>> *Nod head yes.*
> Creating the world,
>> *Stretch arms wide.*
> Sending Jesus, His Son.
>> *Form cross with index fingers.*
>
> I say thank You to God
>> *Fold hands.*
> For all that I see.
>> *Shade eyes with hand.*
> I say thanks most of all
>> *Fold hands.*
> For His love for me.
>> *Hug self.*

Harvest Time: Take off your child's shoes and socks (and yours too!) and use fingers and toes to count God's blessings.

My Prayer: Dear God, thank You for all the good things You give me. Thanks especially for *(ask your child to name some things)*. In Jesus' name. Amen.

16

Going to God's House

The Seed: I rejoiced with those who said to me, "Let us go to the house of the LORD." *Psalm 122:1*

Planting Time

>I will jump, jump for joy
>>*Jump in place.*
>
>When to God's house we go.
>>*Press fingertips together to form a steeple.*
>
>I will clap, clap my hands
>>*Clap.*
>
>When I see the church I know.
>>*Press fingertips together to form a steeple.*

>I will hop, hop around
>>*Hop in place.*
>
>When to God's house we go.
>>*Press fingertips together to form a steeple.*
>
>I will shout, shout "hurray"
>>*Shout "hurray!"*
>
>When I see the church I know.
>>*Press fingertips together to form a steeple.*

Harvest Time: Take your child to visit your church during the week. Explore together, answering your child's questions. Discuss things you can look for during worship—the cross on the altar, the candles being lit, the baptismal font, people sharing God's special meal, etc. Teach your child some of the simple refrains used in your church's liturgy and music.

My Prayer: Thank You, God, for my church. I like to visit Your house! In Jesus' name. Amen.

Jesus Is at My House!

The Seed: "Zacchaeus, come down. ... I must stay at your house today." *Luke 19:5*

Planting Time

> If I were small Zacchaeus,
> I know what I would say.
> I'd jump and sing and shout "Hurray!"
> If Jesus came today.
>
> I'd pick my favorite toys
> So He and I could play.
> I'd plan a special snack for Him
> If Jesus came today.
>
> Remember what He promised,
> That He's with us every day?
> I'll jump and sing and shout "Hurray!"
> 'Cause Jesus is here today!

Harvest Time: As you share God's Word and your love for Jesus, God's Holy Spirit will work through you to strengthen your young child's faith. Be sure there are tangible reminders of Jesus' presence in your home—a cross, a picture of Jesus with children, your Bible and Bible storybooks. Prepare a special snack together. Pray before you eat, thanking Jesus for being a member of your household.

My Prayer: Jesus, I can't see You, but I know You are always with me. Thank You. Amen.

18

Jesus Is My Light

The Seed: I am the light of the world. *John 8:12*

Planting Time: *Light a candle as you say this poem with your child.*

> Jesus is my Savior,
> My bright and shining light.
> He takes away the darkness
> Like a candle in the night.
>
> When I do something wrong
> That makes me feel so sad,
> I tell Jesus all about it,
> And then He makes me glad.

Harvest Time: Tell your child that our sins—the bad things we do—make us live in the dark. But Jesus died to pay the price of our sin. He is the light that brightens our darkness. Choose a special candle to light for your family devotion time. Let your child play with a flashlight and see how it brightens up a dark room. Plan on counting the candles you see at church during worship.

My Prayer: Jesus, thank You for taking my sins away. Thank You for being my light. Amen.

Growing Good Food

The Seed: [God] provides you with plenty of food.
Acts 14:17

Planting Time

> I plant a little seed
> *Hold "seed" in fingertips.*
> Down deep in the ground.
> *Pat the ground.*
> God waters it with rain,
> *Wiggle fingers for raindrops.*
> Sends sunshine all around.
> *Spread arms wide.*
>
> Soon God makes a plant,
> *Point at "plant."*
> Stretching tall as can be,
> *Raise your hands from the floor to
> above your head.*
> Growing some good food
> *Rub tummy.*
> For you and for me.
> *Point to each other, then to self.*

Harvest Time: Tell your child that God helps seeds grow so we always will have good food to eat. Plant quick-growing seeds—beans, pumpkins, radishes—with your child. Use a flowerpot if you can't plant seeds outside.

My Prayer: Dear God, thank You for sending rain and sunshine to help seeds grow. Thank You for the food I eat. In Jesus' name. Amen.

Loving and Obeying

The Seed: This is love for God: to obey His commands.
1 John 5:3

Planting Time

> I love God in a great big way.
> > *Stretch arms wide.*
> I know just what I'll do.
> > *Nod head yes.*
> I'll learn what He tells me in His Word,
> > *Form open book with hands.*
> And I'll obey it too.
> > *Nod head yes.*
>
> God's commands are not too hard;
> > *Shake head no.*
> Jesus helps me to obey.
> > *Form cross with index fingers.*
> Mom and Dad will help me too,
> > *Point to Mom and Dad.*
> Loving God in a great big way.
> > *Stretch arms wide.*

Harvest Time: Talk with your child about some of God's commands that she can understand—obey parents, love one another, be kind, pray for one another, etc. Say, "We can't always obey every command just right, but Jesus loves us and helps us." Ask your child to choose a special command. Write the command—using a short, simple phrase—with crayon or marker on a large sheet of paper. Let your child sprinkle glitter on the letters or outline them with colored glue. Celebrate each time Jesus helps a family member obey that command.

My Prayer: Dear God, I love You in a great big way. Please help me to obey Your commands. In Jesus' name. Amen.

I Will Be a Friend

The Seed: Serve one another in love. *Galatians 5:13*

Harvest Time

> I will be a friend
> > *Nod head yes.*
> When someone's feeling sad.
> > *Make a sad face.*
> I'll try to cheer them up
> > *Smile.*
> So they don't feel so bad.
> > *Hug self.*
>
> I will be a friend.
> > *Nod head yes.*
> God's Word I will obey—
> > *Form open book with hands.*
> Sharing love and helping
> > *Cross hands over heart.*
> Every single day.
> > *Nod head yes.*

Harvest Time: Help your child think of someone who needs loving service. You might make a card for a friend at church who is ill; write a note to your pastor, thanking him for sharing God's love; make a picture for Grandma; make a brother's or sister's bed; pick up leaves and sticks on a neighbor's lawn; etc. Tell your child that Jesus fills us with love and helps us love other people.

My Prayer: Dear Jesus, show me who needs some special love today and help me to serve them. Amen.

A Big Catch

The Seed: It is the Lord! *John 21:7*

Planting Time: *Read John 21:4–7a with your child. Explain how Jesus' helpers caught fish by throwing a large net into the water. (You might want to throw a small blanket out on the floor and gather it up.) Then act out this poem.*

> The disciples rowed and rowed their boat
> > *Pretend to row boat.*
> And fished all through the night.
> > *Pretend to cast net into water.*
> But when they pulled the nets back in,
> > *Pretend to pull net into boat.*
> There were no fish inside.
> > *Shake head no.*
>
> Someone on the shore called out
> > *Cup hands to mouth.*
> And asked them what they'd caught.
> > *Hold palms up in questioning gesture.*
> He told them, "Put the net back out,"
> > *Cup hands to mouth.*
> And they'd find the fish they sought.
> > *Nod head yes.*
>
> They threw the net back in the sea.
> > *Pretend to cast net into water.*
> Suddenly—it was full!
> > *Gasp in surprise.*

There were more fish in the net
Spread arms wide.
Than all of them could pull.
Pretend to pull heavy net in.

Harvest Time: Enjoy a snack of goldfish crackers. Ask your child who he thinks helped the disciples. Explain that Jesus is always ready to help us. Take turns acting out the story using your blanket-net. Your child can be a disciple, Jesus, even a fish!

My Prayer: Dear Jesus, thank You for helping me with everything I need. Amen.

Lights at Night

The Seed: God said, "Let there be lights in ... the sky."
Genesis 1:14

Planting Time

> I see the stars
> > *Point up.*
> Twinkling at me.
> > *Wiggle fingers like twinkling stars.*
> I see the moon
> > *Point up.*
> Shining for me.
> > *Circle arms overhead.*
>
> God made the moon
> > *Point up.*
> To give me soft light.
> > *Circle arms overhead.*
> God made the stars
> > *Point up.*
> To light the dark night.
> > *Wiggle fingers like twinkling stars.*

Harvest Time: If possible, take your child outside at night to look at the moon and the stars. Thank God for making such a beautiful world for us to enjoy. Tape glow-in-the-dark stars on the ceiling in your child's room so she can thank God for lights in the sky when she goes to bed.

My Prayer: Thank You, God, for making the stars and the moon. In Jesus' name. Amen.

Sharing God's Love

The Seed: Share with others. *Hebrews 13:16*

Planting Time

> I'll share my ball.
> > *Pretend to bounce ball.*
> I'll share my doll.
> > *Pretend to rock doll.*
> I'll share with you—
> > *Point to each other.*
> Today!
> > *Clap hands.*
>
> I'll share my seat.
> > *Pat chair or ground.*
> I'll share my treat.
> > *Rub tummy.*
> I'll share with you—
> > *Point to each other.*
> Today!
> > *Clap hands.*

Harvest Time: Tell your child "Thank you for sharing" often. When you are enjoying a treat or reading a book, say, "Let me share with you." Explain that we can share God's love by being kind to others. Help your child to pick a toy to share with children in your church nursery or at a hospital or shelter.

My Prayer: God, help me to share the good things You give me. In Jesus' name. Amen.

Follow Me

The Seed: "Follow Me." *Matthew 9:9*

Planting Time: *Tell your child the story of Jesus calling Matthew (Matthew 9:9–13). Then enjoy this poem together.*

> When Jesus said to Matthew,
> > *Place finger on lips.*
> "Come and follow Me,"
> > *Make a beckoning motion.*
> Matthew got up and followed
> > *Walk in place.*
> As quick as one, two, three.
> > *Count to three on fingers.*
>
> I like to follow Jesus
> > *Nod head yes.*
> Like Matthew did that day.
> > *Walk in place.*
> I like to follow Jesus
> > *Nod head yes.*
> In all I do and say.
> > *Walk in place.*

Harvest Time: Play a simple game of "Follow the Leader." Explain that we follow Jesus when we love Him, tell people about Him, and act like Him. Act out some loving deeds—share, hug, say "Jesus loves you." Thank each other for following Jesus.

My Prayer: Dear Jesus, I love You. Help me to follow You. Amen.

Sweeter than Honey

The Seed: How sweet are Your words to my taste, sweeter than honey to my mouth! *Psalm 119:103*

Planting Time: *Enjoy a snack of honey on bread or crackers while you say this poem with your child.*

> When my parents and my teachers
> And my pastor talk to me,
> They tell me all about God's Word
> And His great love for me.
>
> God tells me how He sent His Son
> To live and die for me.
> I'll keep His teachings in my heart
> And listen carefully.

Harvest Time: Look at your family Bible with your child. Explain that we know this book is true because it is God's Word. In it God tells us He loves us so much that He sent His Son to die for us. God helps us share that big love with one another. Honey is a sweet treat that we like to eat. God's Word is full of Good News that we like to hear and share.

My Prayer: Dear God, thank You for telling us the Good News about Jesus. Amen.

God Is Patient

The Seed: [God] is patient with you. *2 Peter 3:9*

Planting Time: *Discuss times when you and your child have had to be patient—waiting in a line, waiting to open birthday presents, waiting for dinner to be ready. Then enjoy this poem together.*

> God is very patient.
> He always waits for me.
> He gives me love in Jesus.
> He loves eternally.
>
> God helps me to be patient,
> To wait and help and share.
> He gives me everything I need
> And keeps me in His care.

Harvest Time: Explain that God is always patient with us. Even though He is displeased with the bad things we do, He lovingly works to turn our hearts around and bring us to repentance. He forgives us because of Jesus and patiently helps us share His love. Say "Thank you for being patient" often to your child when he has waited patiently for something.

My Prayer: Dear God, help me to be patient like You. In Jesus' name. Amen.

Jesus Is My Brother

The Seed: Love as brothers. *1 Peter 3:8*

Planting Time

> Jesus is my brother;
> > *Cross hands over heart.*
> He gave His life for me.
> > *Form cross with index fingers.*
> He helps me love my family
> > *Hug each other.*
> And everyone I see.
> > *Spread arms wide.*

Harvest Time: Explain to your child that she became part of God's family when she was baptized. Look at baptism pictures together. Say, "Now Jesus is your brother." Talk about your child's brother or a friend who has brothers. Say the love that Jesus gives us is even bigger than the love that brothers share.

My Prayer: God, thank You for making me part of Your family. I love my brother Jesus. Amen.

God Keeps an Eye on Me

The Seed: You know when I sit and when I rise.
Psalm 139:2

Planting Time

> If I climb the highest mountain
> > *Pretend to climb.*
> Or swim the ocean blue,
> > *Pretend to swim.*
> If I run along the sidewalk,
> > *Run in place.*
> God sees just what I do.
> > *Point up.*

> Each day when I play,
> > *Point to self.*
> Each night when I sleep,
> > *Rest cheek on hands.*
> God watches and loves me,
> > *Point up.*
> In safety to keep.
> > *Hug self.*

Harvest Time: Discuss all the things you and your child have done today. Explain that God loves us so much that He is always with us, watching us and keeping us safe. Play a question-and-answer game with your child. Does God see me at Grandma's house? Does God see me when I ride my tricycle? The answer is always yes!

My Prayer: Dear God, I'm glad You're always with me. In Jesus' name. Amen.

God Can Do Anything

The Seed: With God all things are possible.
Matthew 19:26

Planting Time: *Clap as you chant this poem with your child.*

> He can heal the sick,
> Even raise the dead,
> And make the lame
> Jump out of bed!
>
> He can make the blind
> See good as new;
> He can meet the needs
> Of me and you!
>
> He makes me happy,
> So I jump and sing.
> My mighty God
> Can do anything!

Harvest Time: Talk about your child's favorite "super-heroes." Explain that their power is make-believe, but God really can do anything. Act out some of the stories of Jesus' healing miracles together.

My Prayer: God, You are so great! You take care of my family and me. You can do anything! In Jesus' name. Amen.

Sometimes I'm Angry

The Seed: In your anger do not sin. *Ephesians 4:26*

Planting Time: *Have fun stamping your feet and frowning as you and your child act out this poem. Explain that the feeling of anger is not bad in itself, but it easily can lead us to hurt someone else or ourselves.*

> Sometimes I get angry
> When things don't go my way,
> When someone hurts my feelings
> Or won't let me play.
>
> Everyone gets angry—
> That feeling is not bad.
> God helps us to be careful
> When we are feeling mad.
>
> I can tell someone I'm angry;
> I can run or jump or sing.
> I can tell God just how I feel—
> He helps with everything.

Harvest Time: Discuss times when you and your child have felt angry. Make a list of things your child can do to release angry feelings—run around the yard, jump up and down, play a physical game. Apologize to your child when anger causes you to say or do hurtful things.

My Prayer: God, help me when I'm angry. In Jesus' name. Amen.

Sometimes I Goof

The Seed: What I do is not the good I want to do. *Romans 7:19*

Planting Time: *Tell your child about a time she will be able to understand when you wanted to do the right thing but slipped up and did something wrong. Then enjoy this poem together.*

> I want to do good things
> To please my mom and dad.
> But sometimes I slip up
> And do things that are bad.
>
> God helps me when I'm bad
> To do the things I should.
> He takes my sins away
> And helps me do what's good.

Harvest Time: Role-play with your child how to say "I'm sorry" to God and to other people. Remember to apologize and ask your child's forgiveness when it's necessary. Say, "God is always happy to forgive us because Jesus took the punishment for our sins." Celebrate God's forgiveness with a special game or treat.

My Prayer: Dear God, I want to be good, but sometimes I'm not. Help me to be good and forgive me when I'm not. In Jesus' name. Amen.

33

Don't Worry

The Seed: Cast your cares on the LORD. *Psalm 55:22*

Planting Time

> God tells me not to worry;
> *Shake head no.*
> He'll take good care of me.
> *Nod head yes.*
> I can love and trust Him
> *Cross hands over heart.*
> And tell Him what I need.
> *Fold hands.*
>
> I talk to God whenever
> *Fold hands.*
> Something troubles me.
> *Frown.*
> Then I don't have to worry—
> *Smile.*
> He gives me what I need.
> *Hold hands out as if receiving a gift.*

Harvest Time: Help your child pick a "prayer corner." Place a comfortable chair or pillow there, as well as a picture of Jesus or a small cross and a children's Bible or some Bible storybooks. Encourage your child to use his prayer corner to talk to God about anything. Remind your child that he may talk to God anytime, anywhere.

My Prayer: Dear God, thank You for listening to me when something is bothering me. In Jesus' name. Amen.

God's Gifts

The Seed: Give ... to God what is God's. *Luke 20:25*

Planting Time

> All that I have
> God's given to me.
> I'll give gifts to Him.
> I'll give cheerfully.
>
> I'll give Him my time
> By helping someone.
> I'll give money too
> So His work can be done.

Harvest Time: Let your child use her time and talents to give God a gift. You might clean your church's nursery or your child's Sunday school room, wash toys used by babies in the nursery, or visit someone who is lonely. Let your child help you prepare your offering envelope. During the offering, give her an offering to give too.

My Prayer: God, thank You for all the things You give me. Show me how to give gifts back to You. In Jesus' name. Amen.

Sad and Happy

The Seed: [God] turned to me and heard my cry.
Psalm 40:1

Planting Time

> I can talk to God
> > *Fold hands.*
> When I am sad.
> > *Frown.*
> He listens to me
> > *Cup hands around ears.*
> And makes me glad.
> > *Smile.*
>
> God knows me best
> > *Point to self.*
> And loves me too.
> > *Cross hands over heart.*
> When I am sad,
> > *Frown.*
> He knows what to do.
> > *Nod head yes.*

Harvest Time: Give your child two paper plates or two circles cut from paper. Help him draw a sad face on one circle and a happy face on the other. Discuss things that make him happy or sad. Let him find the correct face for each example. Say, "We can talk to God whether we are happy or sad. When we are sad God knows how to help us and make us feel happy again."

My Prayer: God, I'm glad I can talk to You when I'm happy or sad. When I'm sad, You make me feel better. In Jesus' name. Amen.

Following Jesus

The Seed: "Come, follow Me," Jesus said, "and I will make you fishers of men." *Mark 1:17*

Planting Time: *Tell your child that when we tell others about Jesus' love and share His love by doing kind things for others, we help to "catch" them for Jesus. Then enjoy this poem together.*

> Following Jesus
> Every day,
> Living for Him
> At home and at play,
>
> Following Jesus
> Shows others the way—
> Fishing for people
> At home and at play.

Harvest Time: Think of some ways your child can give a faith witness: Share a Bible storybook with a friend and invite that child to Sunday school. Make a card about Jesus' love for someone who is sick. Pray together before having lunch or a snack with playmates.

My Prayer: Dear Jesus, please help me "catch" people for You by sharing Your love. Amen.

Best Friends

The Seed: A friend loves at all times. *Proverbs 17:17*

Planting Time

> Jesus is my friend.
> He loves me all the time.
> I love *(ask your child to name a friend)*
> Because she's (he's) a friend of mine.

Harvest Time: Say, "Jesus is your very best friend. He loves you so much that He gave His life for you. Jesus helps you share His love with your friends." Let your child make something for a friend—cookies or frosted graham crackers, a picture, etc.

My Prayer: Thank You, Jesus, for being my best friend. Help me share Your love with all of my friends. Amen.

God Cares for Me

The Seed: The … hairs of your head are all numbered.
Matthew 10:30

Planting Time: *Pretend to count the hairs on your head and on your child's head. Decide that there are too many to count. Explain that God takes such good care of us that He even knows the number of hairs on our heads. Then enjoy this poem together.*

> God has counted
> The hairs on my head—
> > *Point to hair.*
> How many there are,
> Black, blond, brown, or red.
>
> God knows the color
> Of my eyes too—
> > *Point to eyes.*
> If they're gray or brown
> Or green or blue.
>
> God knows where I sleep
> And where I play.
> God cares for me
> > *Point to self.*
> Every day.

Harvest Time: Help your child draw a picture of herself. Decide which colors to use for hair, eyes, and skin. Write the Bible verse on the picture and display it on the refrigerator with a photograph of your child.

My Prayer: Dear God, I'm so glad that You know all about me. Thank You for taking good care of me. In Jesus' name. Amen.

Angry Faces

The Seed: A gentle answer turns away [anger].
Proverbs 15:1

Planting Time

> When someone is angry
> And looks so mad,
> *Make an angry face.*
> Saying unkind words
> Makes everyone sad.
> *Make a sad face.*
>
> When someone is angry
> For a little while,
> *Make an angry face.*
> I'll use kind words
> And make them smile!
> *Smile.*

Harvest Time: Explain that using kind words can help others when they are angry. Role-play situations in which someone is angry. Choose kind words that might help. For example, if a friend is angry because his blocks got knocked down, your child could say, "Let me help you build your wall again."

My Prayer: Dear God, help me to use kind words when others are angry. In Jesus' name. Amen.

Jesus Shows the Way

The Seed: In My Father's house are many rooms. … I am going there to prepare a place for you. *John 14:2*

Planting Time: *Show your child a picture of Jesus blessing the children. Say, "Heaven will be a wonderful place because we will get to talk with Jesus all the time." Then enjoy this poem together.*

> Heaven is the home
> I'm going to some day
> To live with Jesus always—
> He shows me the way.

Harvest Time: Talk with your child about how wonderful it is that Jesus has opened heaven to us by dying on the cross to pay for our sins and rising again on the first Easter. Let your child help prepare your home for a guest in some way—help prepare food, make a centerpiece for the table, draw a welcome sign, etc.

My Prayer: Dear Jesus, thank You for getting my room in heaven ready. Amen.

When I'm Afraid

The Seed: I will fear no evil, for You are with me.
Psalm 23:4

Planting Time

> I'm never alone
> Wherever I go.
> In dark, scary places,
> God's with me, I know.
>
> When I get scared,
> I know that God's near,
> Holding my hand—
> I have nothing to fear.

Harvest Time: Discuss some places that seem frightening to your child. Discuss how God takes care of us in each of those places. Then discuss some fun places—the park, McDonald's, the backyard, preschool, etc. Tell your child that God takes good care of her in those places too.

My Prayer: God, I am so glad that You take care of me in scary places and in fun places. In Jesus' name. Amen.

Seeing Jesus

The Seed: This is how God showed His love among us: He sent His one and only Son. *1 John 4:9*

Planting Time

> I can't see God.
> He's invisible, you see.
> But I know all about Him
> Because Jesus lives in me.
>
> God sent His Son, Jesus,
> To live upon the earth.
> That's why we have Christmas—
> To celebrate His birth.
>
> Jesus showed His love for me
> By dying for my sin.
> Now I'll go to heaven
> And live someday with Him.

Harvest Time: Tell your child that even though we can't see God, we know what He is like because He tells us about Himself in the Bible. Read some stories about Jesus with your child and think of words that describe Him—kind, loving, a good friend, etc.

My Prayer: Dear Jesus, I can see what You're like by learning what You did. Thank You for loving me so much. Amen.

God Is So Good

The Seed: I will sing to the LORD, for He has been good to me. *Psalm 13:6*

Planting Time

> God takes care of me.
> > *Point to self.*
> God takes care of you.
> > *Point to each other.*
> That makes me so happy,
> > *Smile.*
> I sing "allelu."
> > *Sing "allelu."*

Harvest Time: Sing some of your child's favorite songs about Jesus. Teach your child a song or liturgical response so you will be able to sing it together during worship.

My Prayer: Dear God, thank You for taking such good care of me. It makes me want to sing! In Jesus' name. Amen.

A Clean Heart

The Seed: Though your sins are like scarlet, they shall be as white as snow. *Isaiah 1:18*

Planting Time: *Cut two hearts—one from red construction paper, the other from white. Tape the hearts together. Show your child the red side. Talk about a time in your family when angry or unkind words were spoken. Explain that feeling angry inside can sometimes make us say and do things that aren't loving. When that happens, we tell Jesus we are sorry. Show your child the white side. Explain that Jesus washes all our sins away and makes us clean as snow. Let your child show the red side of the heart for the first stanza, then show the white side for the second stanza.*

> Unkind words or naughty words,
> Words that shouldn't start,
> Words that hurt when others hear,
> Come from an angry heart.
>
> Jesus takes those words away,
> Makes me clean as snow,
> Helps me use the loving words
> That make big smiles grow.

Harvest Time: Help your child cut several hearts from white paper. Think of loving things that are said often around your house: I love you. You're a good helper. Please and thank you. Write these phrases on the hearts and let your child hang them on the refrigerator with magnets.

My Prayer: Dear God, I'm sorry that I sometimes say and do things that hurt others. Thank You for making me clean as snow. In Jesus' name. Amen.

I'm Sorry

The Seed: Wash away all my [sin]. *Psalm 51:2*

Planting Time: *Say this stanza with a sad face.*

> When I have sinned—
> Done something wrong—
> It makes me sad
> The whole day long.

Fold your hands during this stanza.

> Then I can go
> To God and pray;
> Tell Him, "I'm sorry.
> Forgive me today."

Say this stanza with a happy face.

> God forgives me
> When I do wrong.
> That makes me happy
> The whole day long.

Harvest Time: Role-play situations in which you or your child pretends to do something wrong. Practice saying "I'm sorry" and "I forgive you." Use these words often in your home.

My Prayer: Dear God, thank You for forgiving me when I sin. In Jesus' name. Amen.

God's Blessings

The Seed: [God] richly blesses all who call on Him.
Romans 10:12

Planting Time

> Just look at all the blessings
> > *Spread arms wide.*
> That God has given me—
> > *Point up.*
> A nice warm house and food to eat
> > *Press fingertips together to form roof,*
> > *then pretend to eat.*
> And all that I can see.
> > *Cup hand over eyes.*
>
> Just look at all the blessings
> > *Spread arms wide.*
> That God has given me—
> > *Point up.*
> A world to share with friends at play,
> > *Make circle with arms.*
> His love, eternally.
> > *Cross hands over heart.*

Harvest Time: Explain that blessings are all the good things that God gives to us. Write the word "Blessings" on a sheet of paper. Let your child draw pictures of blessings, or cut pictures from magazines, to make a blessings poster. Display the poster and thank God for the blessings pictured when you pray together.

My Prayer: God, thank You for all Your blessings to me, especially *(ask your child to name some blessings)*. In Jesus' name. Amen.

Secret Love

The Seed: Your Father, who sees what is done in secret, will reward you. *Matthew 6:4*

Planting Time

> I'll be a secret helper,
> > *Place finger on lips.*
> Not telling what I do;
> > *Shake head no.*
> Always helping others
> > *Nod head yes.*
> Maybe I'll help you!
> > *Point to each other.*

Harvest Time: Tell your child that we don't need to show off about being kind to others. God thanks us for sharing His love—even when we do it secretly. Plan a secret good deed to do with your child—leave flowers or cookies on a neighbor's porch; write a letter to Grandma, but don't sign it; etc.

My Prayer: Dear God, I want to be a secret helper. Please show me what to do. In Jesus' name. Amen.

Praying for Others

The Seed: Pray for each other. *James 5:16*

Planting Time

> If I know someone who's hungry,
>> *Rub tummy.*
> Hurt or sad or sick,
>> *Make a sad face.*
> I'll ask my God to help them.
>> *Point up.*
> I'll pray for them so quick.
>> *Fold hands.*
>
> God cares for all His people;
>> *Spread arms wide.*
> He hears me when I pray.
>> *Point to ears.*
> I'll tell Him of the needs of those
>> *Fold hands.*
> That I have seen today.
>> *Point to eyes.*

Harvest Time: Explain that besides praying about the things we need, God asks us to pray for others as well. Help your child think of acquaintances or people you have seen who need your prayers—friends, family members, a homeless person, a person in an ambulance, etc. Pray together, then think of some ways you can help the people you prayed for—take food or clothing to a shelter, make a card for someone who is in the hospital, etc.

My Prayer: Dear God, I am glad that I can pray to You about anyone who needs Your help. In Jesus' name. Amen.

God's Gift to Us

The Seed: A Savior has been born to you; He is Christ the Lord. *Luke 2:11*

Planting Time

Shepherds were watching
> *Cup hand over eyes and look around.*

Their sheep in the night
> *Rest cheek on hands.*

When an angel appeared
> *Hold arms out in greeting.*

And gave them a fright.
> *Gasp in surprise.*

"Do not be afraid,"
> *Shake head no.*

The angel did say.
> *Touch finger to lips.*

"Jesus, your Savior,
> *Form cross with index finger.*

Is born on this day."
> *Rock a baby.*

The shepherds ran off
> *Run in place.*

To find Joseph and Mary,
> *Cup hand over eyes and look around.*

And there was Jesus,
> *Point to a "manger."*

A tiny baby.
> *Rock a baby.*

God sent us His Son
    Point up.
That first Christmas day
    Hold up index finger.
To save us from sin.
    Form cross with index fingers.
Let's shout "hurray!"
    Shout "hurray!"

The Harvest: Emphasize to your child that Jesus was born just like she was. Mary and Joseph had to take care of the baby, and Jesus had to learn to walk and talk just like she did. But Jesus was special. He was God's Son. He never did anything wrong. God sent Jesus to be our Savior from sin. Because of Jesus, God forgives us for the wrong things we do. Sing some familiar Christmas carols with your child (even if it's July!) and celebrate Jesus' birth with a special snack.

My Prayer: God, thank You for sending Jesus to be my Savior. He's the best Christmas present ever. Amen.

Feelings

The Seed: Rejoice with those who rejoice; mourn with those who mourn. *Romans 12:15*

Planting Time: *Draw a happy face on one paper plate and a sad face on another. Let your child hold the happy face for the first stanza of the poem and the sad face for the second.*

> When you are very happy
> And God sends blessings to you,
> I'll tell you, "That's terrific!"
> And I'll be happy too.
>
> When something bothers you
> And you are feeling bad,
> I'll put my arms around you
> And tell you I am sad.

Harvest Time: Think of a family member or friend who has experienced a special blessing. Have your child dictate a note expressing joy for that person. Then think of someone who needs your sympathy and write that person a note as well. You might want to take your child with you to the post office to mail the notes or hand deliver them.

My Prayer: God, thank You for my family and friends. Let me be happy when they are happy and be helpful when they are sad. In Jesus' name. Amen.

God Cares

The Seed: He cares for you. *1 Peter 5:7*

Planting Time

> God cares for you.
> > *Point to each other.*
> God cares for me,
> > *Point to self.*
> God cares for all
> > *Spread arms wide.*
> His family.
> > *Hold hands.*

Harvest Time: Cut pictures of people from catalogs and magazines and make a collage. If your child is not using scissors, cut out the pictures ahead of time and help your child glue them to a sheet of paper. Include snapshots of family members. Discuss how God cares for each of you.

My Prayer: Thank You, God, for caring for me. Thank You for caring for *(ask your child to name family members)*. In Jesus' name. Amen.

Out, Out, Out!

The Seed: Rid yourselves of all such things.
Colossians 3:8

Planting Time

> They're going out, out, out!
> > *Point thumb over shoulder.*
> You won't find them here.
> > *Cup hand over eyes and look around.*
> No angry words or hurting others,
> > *Shake head no.*
> No naughty talk you'll hear.
> > *Place finger over lips.*
>
> They're going out, out, out!
> > *Point thumb over shoulder.*
> You won't find them here.
> > *Cup hand over eyes and look around.*
> Jesus helps me throw them out.
> > *Point thumb over shoulder.*
> They are nowhere near.
> > *Shake head no.*

Harvest Time: Use a paintbrush or squeeze bottle to paint with water on the sidewalk. Watch the water disappear. Tell your child that Jesus helps make the naughty things in our life disappear. He will help us share His love instead of hurting others. When we forget, He will forgive us and help us to do better the next time. Think of a hurtful action that you and your child would like to ask Jesus to help you throw out. Then pray together.

My Prayer: Dear God, help me throw out naughty words and bad temper from my life. In Jesus' name. Amen.

53

Jesus Is Powerful

The Seed: He commands even the winds and the water, and they obey Him. *Luke 8:25*

Planting Time: *Rock from side to side as your child repeats the first stanza, line for line, after you.*

> A boat rocked on the water.
> A boat rocked on the sea.
> Jesus and His helpers
> Were leaving Galilee.
>
> Jesus was sleeping soundly;
> > *Rest cheek on hands.*
> The disciples rowed the boat.
> > *Pretend to row boat.*
> Then the wind and rain came up—
> > *Rock vigorously.*
> They could hardly stay afloat!
> > *Continue to rock.*
>
> The disciples woke up Jesus.
> > *Stretch as if just awakening.*
> "Help!" they cried to Him.
> > *Cup hands around mouth.*
> He told the wind and waves to stop,
> > *Hold palm out in a commanding manner.*
> And all was quiet again.
> > *Rock gently from side to side.*

Harvest Time: Act out this story with your child, using a pan, sink, or tub full of water and a toy boat or small plastic container. Let your child make waves with his hand and blow the boat. Then tell him to be like Jesus and tell the wind and waves to stop. Tell your child that Jesus is so powerful, He will keep him safe always.

My Prayer: Thank You, Jesus, for taking such good care of me. Amen.

Who Is Jesus?

The Seed: "You are the Christ, the Son of the living God." *Matthew 16:16*

Planting Time: *Sing this poem with your child to the tune of "Are You Sleeping?"*

> Who is Jesus? Who is Jesus?
> He's my friend; He's my friend.
> He's my friend and Savior, Son of God,
> Redeemer.
> He's my friend; He's my friend.

Harvest Time: Help your child list all the places she can learn about Jesus—from God's Word, at church, in Sunday school, from Mom and Dad, etc. Read some of your child's favorite stories about Jesus. Help her make a special picture of Jesus to hang over her bed.

My Prayer: God, thank You for sending Jesus to be my Savior and friend. Amen.

Pay Back Wrong with Good

The Seed: Make sure that nobody pays back wrong for wrong, but always try to be kind to each other. *1 Thessalonians 5:15*

Planting Time

> When someone hurts me,
> > *Make a sad face.*
> That is wrong.
> > *Shake finger.*
> But I won't hurt back—
> > *Shake head no.*
> I'll be strong.
> > *Flex arm muscles.*
>
> Strong to do
> > *Flex arm muscles.*
> Just as God said:
> > *Touch finger to lips.*
> Don't pay back wrong;
> > *Shake head no.*
> Do good instead.
> > *Nod head yes.*

Harvest Time: Role-play a situation in which someone might hurt your child. Help your child understand the things he can do to handle the situation: Tell the other child to stop. Tell an adult what is happening. Go away from the situation. Remind your child that Jesus is always with him to help him handle things. Have your child help you "do good" for someone—make a small gift or treat to take on a visit, invite someone to play, etc.

My Prayer: God, when people hurt me, help me to be strong enough not to hurt them back. Help me to do good to others. In Jesus' name. Amen.

God Made It All

The Seed: The earth is the LORD'S, and everything in it.
Psalm 24:1

Planting Time

> From the great, wide ocean
> > *Spread arms wide.*
> To the mountain tall
> > *Raise palms above head.*
> To the grassy plain,
> > *Pat the ground.*
> God made it all.
> > *Point up.*
>
> From the itty, bitty bug
> > *Walk fingers up arm.*
> To the great big tree,
> > *Stretch arms up for branches.*
> God made it all,
> > *Point up.*
> Even *(insert Mom, Dad, or name of friend)*,
> even me!
> > *Point to self.*

Harvest Time: Discuss the importance of caring for God's creation. Let your child help sort recyclables, plant some seeds, hang a bird feeder, or take care of a pet.

My Prayer: Dear God, thank You for giving us such a wonderful world. In Jesus' name. Amen.

Looking Good!

The Seed: Listen, my son, to your father's instruction and do not forsake your mother's teaching. They will be a garland to grace your head and a chain to adorn your neck. *Proverbs 1:8–9*

Planting Time: *Help your child string cereal, macaroni, or beads to make a necklace as you enjoy this poem.*

> If I listen to my dad,
> I'm looking good!
> If I listen to my dad,
> I'm looking good!
>
> If I remember what Mom says,
> I'm looking good!
> If I remember what Mom says,
> I'm looking good!

Harvest Time: Let your child wear the necklace as a reminder that listening to Mom and Dad will help her shine with Jesus' love.

My Prayer: Dear God, help me listen to Mom and Dad and do what they say. In Jesus' name. Amen.

Be a Light

The Seed: Let your light shine before men, that they may see your good deeds and praise your Father in heaven. *Matthew 5:16*

Planting Time: *Light a candle as you enjoy this poem with your child.*

> The light of Jesus shines in me,
> Shining bright for all to see.
> I would never hide my light;
> Jesus keeps it shining bright.

Harvest Time: Explain to your child that Jesus is our shining light—He takes away the darkness of the wrong things we do and shows us the way to heaven. Jesus puts the light of His love in us to help us shine for other people. Help your child think of some ways to let Jesus' light shine—tell a friend who is lonely about Jesus, invite a friend to a family devotion, etc. Play with a flashlight in a darkened room as you sing "This Little Gospel Light of Mine."

My Prayer: Dear Jesus, thank You for showing me the way to heaven. Keep your light shining bright in me. Amen.

I Love Jesus Best

The Seed: God knows your hearts. *Luke 16:15*

Planting Time

> It's no secret to God
> *Shake head no.*
> What's inside of me.
> *Place hands over heart.*
> Whatever I think,
> *Point to head.*
> God can clearly see.
> *Nod head yes.*
>
> Money and toys,
> *Count two fingers.*
> And all the rest,
> *Spread arms wide.*
> Don't matter to me—
> *Shake head no.*
> I love Jesus best!
> *Form cross with index fingers.*

Harvest Time: Have fun listing things that you and your child love—ice cream, teddy bears, Sesame Street, etc. Then discuss the great love Jesus has for us. Explain that because Jesus loves us so much, we overflow with love for Him.

My Prayer: Jesus, I love You best! Amen.

Talking to God

The Seed: To the LORD I cry aloud, and He answers me from His holy hill. *Psalm 3:4*

Planting Time

> I'll talk to God
> *Point up.*
> Each and every day.
> *Nod head yes.*
> I know He hears me
> *Point to ears.*
> When I pray.
> *Fold hands.*

Harvest Time: God loves to hear His children pray and promises to hear every prayer. In His wisdom, God always knows what is best for us and answers our prayers in ways that give us eternal benefits. It is enough for your child to understand that God listens and is concerned about each petition she brings to Him. Help your child think through some phrases for a new prayer that your family can pray together at mealtime.

My Prayer: Thank You, God, for always listening to me. I like to talk to You. In Jesus' name. Amen.

Acting in Love

The Seed: Even a child is known by his actions. *Proverbs 20:11*

Planting Time: *Help your child draw a happy face on one paper plate and a sad face on another as you enjoy this poem.*

> I can share God's love
> In what I say and do.
> Others see my love,
> And they act lovingly too.

Harvest Time: Role-play situations with your child—sharing a toy, throwing a toy in anger, etc. Ask your child to hold up the happy face if the situation shows a way to share God's love or the sad face if the situation does not show a loving action. Explain that our loving words and actions can help others learn what God's love is like. God is always ready to help us share His love.

My Prayer: God, help me share Your love in what I say and in what I do. In Jesus' name. Amen.

God Is My Teacher

The Seed: [God] guides the humble in what is right and teaches them His way. *Psalm 25:9*

Planting Time: *Gather your Bible and some of your child's favorite Bible storybooks and Sunday school lessons. Enjoy looking at them together, then share this poem.*

> I want to do
> What's right and good.
> I want to do
> Just what I should.
>
> Sometimes I don't
> Know what to do—
> The right from wrong
> Is hard to choose.
>
> God tells me what
> I need to know.
> His Word is clear;
> It helps me grow.

Harvest Time: Let your child hold your family Bible. Explain that God gave us His Word so we can learn how Jesus died to save us. In His Word God also teaches us how to love one another. He gives moms and dads the job of teaching their children about His love. Talk about some situations in which your child needs to make a decision or live out his faith—should he take a friend's toy, should he help Dad set the table, should he be careful to obey your warning to stay out of the street, should he put his nickel in the offering, etc.

My Prayer: Dear God, thank You for teaching me what I need to know. In Jesus' name. Amen.

I Love Jesus

The Seed: Whoever has My commands and obeys them, he is the one who loves Me. *John 14:21*

Planting Time

> I love Jesus, yes I do—
> *Nod head yes.*
> That is what I say.
> *Point to mouth.*
> And I can show my love for Him
> *Cross hands over heart.*
> By what I do today.
> *Stretch out arms with palms up.*
>
> I love Jesus, yes I do—
> *Nod head yes.*
> I'll prove it every day.
> *Pound fist on palm.*
> He'll help me share His love
> *Cross hands over heart.*
> While I work and play.
> *Stretch out arms with palms up.*

Harvest Time: Read some of Jesus' commands—John 15:12; Matthew 7:12; Matthew 22:37—with your child and explain them in a simple way. Discuss how your child and your family can live out your love for Jesus. Thank your child when she obeys Jesus' commands and shares His love.

My Prayer: Jesus, I love You. Help me show that love by obeying Your commands. Amen.

Good News

The Seed: Believe the Good News! *Mark 1:15*

Planting Time

> I have Good News,
> > *Point to self with thumbs.*
> Good News to share,
> > *Cup hands around mouth.*
> About Jesus Christ,
> > *Form cross with index fingers.*
> His love and care.
> > *Cross hands over heart.*
>
> I have Good News,
> > *Point to self with thumbs.*
> Good News to share—
> > *Cup hands around mouth.*
> Jesus gave His life
> > *Form cross with index fingers.*
> For all, everywhere.
> > *Spread arms wide.*

Harvest Time: Help your child use a marker to write "Jesus" and draw a cross on a sheet of newspaper. If your child is too young to understand Jesus' sacrifice on the cross, simply say, "A cross reminds us of how much Jesus loves us." Display your Good News newspaper as a witnessing tool to help you say "Jesus loves you" to visitors.

My Prayer: Dear God, thank You for sending Jesus to die for me. Help me share that Good News with others. In Jesus' name. Amen.

I'm a Child of God

The Seed: Whoever believes and is baptized will be saved. *Mark 16:16*

Planting Time

> "He who believes and is baptized
> *Cross hands over heart.*
> Shall be My child," God said.
> *Pretend to rock baby.*
> I do believe and am baptized,
> *Cross hands over heart.*
> By God to heaven I'm led.
> *Point up.*

Harvest Time: Tell your child the story of Jesus' baptism. Then look at pictures of your child's baptism. Talk about that special day and how you celebrated it. Plan to have a special celebration on your child's next baptismal birthday.

My Prayer: Dear God, thank You for making me Your child. In Jesus' name. Amen.

Sing, Sing, Sing

The Seed: Sing psalms, hymns and spiritual songs with gratitude in your hearts to God. *Colossians 3:16*

Planting Time: *Listen to one of your child's favorite recordings of Christian music. March together as you chant this poem. Beat the rhythm by playing some of your child's musical instruments or banging spoons on lids.*

> I've got so much to be thankful for;
> I will sing, sing, sing.
> God's given me food, a home, and more;
> I will sing, sing, sing.
>
> I'll tell Him thanks for my family;
> I will sing, sing, sing.
> I'll tell Him thanks for making me;
> I will sing, sing, sing.

Harvest Time: Sing some of your child's favorite songs from church and Sunday school together. Help him make up a song of his own. Use that song as a bedtime prayer.

My Prayer: God, thank You for being such a great God. I like to sing to You! In Jesus' name. Amen.

Jesus Came Alive

The Seed: We believe that Jesus died and rose again.
1 Thessalonians 4:14

Planting Time: *As you say the first stanza with your child, flutter your hands to show leaves falling and slowly crouch down on the ground.*

> In the fall the leaves
> Drop from the trees,
> And every branch looks dead.

As you say the next stanza, slowly stand up straight with your fingers reaching for the sky.

> In the spring the trees
> Grow brand-new leaves
> And come to life again.

Harvest Time: If possible, plant some flower bulbs (daffodils, tulips, hyacinth, crocus) with your child. They can be planted outside or indoors in a pot. As you bury the bulbs, tell your child that the bulbs look dead, but they will come to life and bear a flower. Explain that Jesus came back to life after He died for us and that, one day, we will come back to life with Him too.

My Prayer: Jesus, I'm glad I'll get to live in heaven with You one day. Amen.

Good Things

The Seed: Every good and perfect gift is from above.
James 1:17

Planting Time

> My home, my food,
> > *Press fingertips together to make a roof.*
> My family—
> > *Hug self.*
> Every good thing,
> > *Nod head yes.*
> God gives to me.
> > *Point up.*
>
> My books, my toys,
> > *Form open book with hands.*
> The things I see—
> > *Point to eyes.*
> Every good thing,
> > *Nod head yes.*
> God gives to me.
> > *Point up.*
>
> The grass outside,
> > *Pat the ground.*
> The shady tree—
> > *Stretch arms overhead.*
> Every good thing,
> > *Nod head yes.*
> God gives to me.
> > *Point up.*

Harvest Time: Help your child cut pictures of things she considers to be good gifts from magazines or catalogs. Glue them to a sheet of paper to make a collage to display. Include a picture of Jesus in the collage.

My Prayer: Thank You, God, for all the good things You give me. Thank You especially for *(ask your child to name some blessings)*. In Jesus' name. Amen.

All That I Do

The Seed: Whatever you do ... do it all in the name of the Lord Jesus. *Colossians 3:17*

Planting Time

>All that I say, all that I do
>>*Point to mouth, then spread arms wide.*
>
>Is done for Jesus' sake.
>>*Form cross with index fingers.*
>
>He loves me and He cares for me
>>*Cross hands over heart.*
>
>As every step I take.
>>*Walk in place.*

Harvest Time: Tell your child that you can thank Jesus for His love in everything you say and do. As you enjoy the rest of your day, thank Jesus often for His love and care. You might say: Look at the good food Jesus gives us to eat—let's thank Him for it. Look at the way you're picking up your toys—Jesus is helping you grow big and strong. Have a nice nap—Jesus will be with you.

My Prayer: Jesus, I like doing things for You. Thank You for loving me. Amen.

My Shepherd

The Seed: I am the Good Shepherd; I know My sheep and My sheep know Me. *John 10:14*

Planting Time: *If your child has a toy lamb, let her hold it while you explain that a shepherd is someone who takes care of sheep and little lambs. Jesus cares for us just like a shepherd cares for his sheep.*

> He cares for them both day and night—
> The shepherd loves His sheep.
> He finds the greenest pastures
> And water, cool and deep.
>
> He cares for me both day and night;
> My shepherd loves me so.
> My shepherd's name is Jesus.
> He watches where I go.

Harvest Time: Help your child make pictures of sheep by gluing cotton balls on paper, then adding legs with a crayon or marker. Discuss all that a shepherd does to take care of the sheep and all that Jesus does to take care of us.

My Prayer: Jesus, You are a good shepherd. Thank You for taking care of me. Amen.

Forgiveness

The Seed: If your brother … repents, forgive him.
Luke 17:4

Planting Time: *Discuss a time when a friend or sibling did something unkind to your child. Give a simple example from your own life of when you have needed to forgive someone who has hurt you. Then enjoy the poem together.*

When someone hurts my feelings
Or breaks a toy of mine,
When someone hits or pushes
Or does something unkind,

I can tell him that it's wrong
To act in that mean way.
But when he says, "I'm sorry,"
I'll forgive and say, "Okay."

It isn't easy to forgive
When friends are mean, you see.
But Jesus helps me do it
By first forgiving me.

Harvest Time: Role-play confessing your sins to Jesus in a very simple way. You might say, "Jesus, I am sorry that I hit my sister." Explain that Jesus forgives us when we do wrong and will help us to forgive others who hurt us. Role-play situations in which your child would need to forgive a friend or sibling.

My Prayer: Jesus, I am so glad that You forgive me when I do wrong things. Help me to forgive others who hurt me. Amen.

Look at the Flowers

The Seed: Why do you worry about clothes? See how the lilies of the field grow. *Matthew 6:28*

Planting Time: *Pick some flowers from your garden or plant a flowering plant or some seeds in a flowerpot as you enjoy this poem.*

The little flowers
Don't worry about clothes—
God dresses them
From their head to their toes.

Some are red
With leaves of green;
Some blue and yellow—
The prettiest you've seen.

Just like the flowers
That I see,
I don't have to worry—
God takes care of me!

Harvest Time: Discuss how God made the beautiful flowers for us to enjoy. The flowers don't need to worry about what to wear or about getting enough sunshine or water. Say, "God loves us even more than He loves the flowers. He will always care for us and be sure we have everything we need."

My Prayer: Thank You, God, for taking care of the flowers. Thank You for taking care of me! In Jesus' name. Amen.

Hurray!

The Seed: Clap your hands ... shout to God with cries of joy. *Psalm 47:1*

Planting Time

> Clap, clap, clap
> > *Clap.*
> And shout hurray!
> > *Shout "hurray!"*
> God loves me
> > *Cross hands over heart.*
> In a great big way.
> > *Spread arms wide.*
>
> Clap, clap, clap,
> > *Clap.*
> And shout hurray!
> > *Shout "hurray!"*
> I love God
> > *Cross hands over heart.*
> In a great big way!
> > *Spread arms wide.*

Harvest Time: Use kitchen utensils and toy instruments to form a rhythm band. Play as you enjoy the poem and sing some favorite Sunday school songs. Make a joyful noise with your child!

My Prayer: God, Your love makes me happy! In Jesus' name. Amen.

The Truth

The Seed: I am the way and the truth and the life. *John 14:6*

Planting Time: *Give your child a silly example of a lie: We have a pet dinosaur in the bathroom. Explain that God's Word is always true. He tells us exactly what we need to know to get to heaven. Let your child hold a Bible or a picture of Jesus while you enjoy this poem.*

When I say
What isn't true,
God sees and hears
Just what I do.

God forgives
For Jesus' sake;
Jesus died,
My sin to take.

Jesus is
The Truth, the Way,
Gives me new life
Every day.

Harvest Time: Enjoy reading some true Bible stories together. Don't worry if your child cannot yet discern between true and fanciful stories. As you continue to share your faith, God's Holy Spirit will leave no doubt in your child's heart as to the truth about Jesus.

My Prayer: Jesus, Your words are always true. Help me to tell the truth. Amen.

God Chose You

The Seed: You are a chosen people. *1 Peter 2:9*

Planting Time: *God chose your child to be His own in his baptism and gives him the job of telling others the Good News of salvation in His Son. You can begin equipping your child for that job as you enjoy this poem together.*

I want to tell you something.
Point to each other.
I have Good News to share:
Nod head yes.
Jesus always loves us;
Form cross with index fingers.
Jesus always cares.
Cross hands over heart.

God chose me to tell you
Point to self.
This Good News that is true:
Nod head yes.
Jesus is my Savior;
Form cross with index fingers.
You need to know him too.
Point to each other.

Harvest Time: Help your child share God's love with someone. Invite a friend to Sunday school, church, or a special event where you will have a chance to witness.

My Prayer: God, I'm glad you picked me to tell the wonderful things You do for us. In Jesus' name. Amen.

God's Name

The Seed: O LORD, our Lord, how majestic is Your name in all the earth! *Psalm 8:1*

Planting Time: *Discuss the names, nicknames, and endearing terms used for family members. Tell your child that we know God by many names too. Then enjoy this poem.*

> Who is God?
> Master, Lord, Jehovah,
> He's called Creator too;
> Ruler of the universe,
> The great I AM is who.
>
> I can call my God by name
> Because He loves me so.
> He calls me *(insert your child's name)*;
> I belong to Him, you know.

Harvest Time: Look for different names for God as you read favorite Bible stories with your child. Listen for different names for God when you worship. If your child is very young, listen for what is most likely her favorite name—Jesus!

My Prayer: God, I'm glad I know Your names and You know mine. In Jesus' name. Amen.

Angels

The Seed: Do not look down on one of these little ones. … [T]heir angels in heaven always see the face of My Father in heaven. *Matthew 18:10*

Planting Time

> I have angels up in heaven,
> > *Point up.*
> Jesus told me so.
> > *Touch finger to lips.*
> They will watch and care for me
> > *Shade eyes with hand.*
> Everywhere I go.
> > *Spread arms wide.*

Harvest Time: Tell your child that God loves him so much that He sends His angels to guard him and keep him safe. Look for pictures of angels with your child. Explain that we can't see angels so we don't know exactly what they look like. In the New Testament they are described as young men wearing bright clothing.

My Prayer: God, thank You for sending Your angels to keep me safe. In Jesus' name. Amen.

Please and Thank You

The Seed: Show ... respect to everyone. *1 Peter 2:17*

Planting Time: *Explain to your child that Jesus lived on earth as a little boy and learned to show respect and treat others with kindness. He helps us show that same respect to others and forgives us when we fail to do so. Enjoy this poem with your child as you practice using good manners.*

> I'll use my please and thank yous
> With everyone I meet.
> I won't forget "Excuse me,"
> If I step on someone's feet.
>
> Jesus helps me show respect;
> He makes me kind and good.
> He makes me glad to share my toys
> And do just as I should.

Harvest Time: Role-play situations in which your child will practice saying "please," "thank you," and "excuse me."

My Prayer: Thank You, Jesus, for helping me to respect others. Please forgive me when I forget. Amen.

Jesus Can

The Seed: What is impossible with men is possible with God. *Luke 18:27*

Planting Time

> Make a bad storm go away?
>> *Hold palms up in a questioning gesture.*
> I can't do that.
>> *Point to self and shake head no.*
> It's impossible!
>> *Pound fist on palm.*
> But Jesus can.
>> *Point up.*
>
> Make a sick person well?
>> *Hold palms up in a questioning gesture.*
> I can't do that.
>> *Point to self and shake head no.*
> It's impossible!
>> *Pound fist on palm.*
> But Jesus can.
>> *Point up.*
>
> Feed many people with five loaves of bread?
>> *Hold palms up in a questioning gesture.*
> I can't do that.
>> *Point to self and shake head no.*
> It's impossible!
>> *Pound fist on palm.*
> But Jesus can.
>> *Point up.*

Harvest Time: Enjoy reading the Bible stories mentioned in the poem with your child. If your child is old enough to understand, explain that Jesus is mightier than any pretend superhero. His miracles show that He is the Son of God and that He does only what is best for us, even to the point of giving His life for us.

My Prayer: Jesus, I'm glad You can take perfect care of me because You are so powerful. Amen.

Jesus Is Coming Again

The Seed: Jesus … will come back in the same way you have seen Him go into heaven. *Acts 1:11*

Planting Time: *Tell your child that after Jesus died and rose again for us, He stayed on earth awhile longer. Then He went to heaven to get our homes ready. As Jesus' disciples looked up into heaven, an angel told them, "Jesus will come back in the same way you saw Him go." Jesus is still with us today, even though we can't see Him. One day He will take us to live with Him in heaven.*

Jesus is coming again someday.
> *Point up.*

It might be tomorrow; it might be today!
> *Hold one palm out, then the other.*

He keeps me ready, living for Him,
> *Nod head yes.*

Forgives me and keeps me free from sin.
> *Form cross with index fingers.*

Jesus is coming again someday.
> *Point up.*

It might be tomorrow; it might be today!
> *Hold one palm out, then the other.*

When I see Him, I'll surely say,
> *Shade eyes with hand.*

"Thank You for helping me every day!"
> *Form cross with index fingers.*

Harvest Time: Tell your child that no one knows when Jesus will come back to earth. It could be very soon or many years from now. In the meantime, we are ready because God's Holy Spirit keeps our faith in Jesus strong. Plan a special celebration with your child to thank Jesus for all He does for us.

My Prayer: Jesus, I'm glad You're coming back someday. Thank You for keeping me ready. Amen.

Doing Good

The Seed: Never tire of doing what is right.
2 Thessalonians 3:13

Planting Time

> I get so tired
> > *Rest cheek on hands.*
>
> When I play,
> > *Clap hands.*
>
> Running and hopping
> > *Run and hop in place.*
>
> All the day.
> > *Spread arms wide.*

> I get so tired
> > *Rest cheek on hands.*
>
> When I pick up toys,
> > *Stoop to pick up toys.*
>
> Or when I have to sit
> > *Sit on floor.*
>
> And not make noise.
> > *Hold finger to lips.*

> But I won't get tired
> > *Shake head no.*
>
> Of doing good.
> > *Clap hands.*
>
> Jesus helps me
> > *Form cross with index fingers.*
>
> Do as I should.
> > *Nod head yes.*

I'll do good things
Clap hands.
For everyone.
Spread arms wide.
I won't get tired,
Shake head no.
Sharing love is fun!
Cross hands over heart.

Harvest Time: Tell your child that, by ourselves, we would not be able to do good things. Jesus fills us with His love and helps us love others. Plan a good deed that you and your child can do for a friend, family member, or even a stranger.

My Prayer: Jesus, thank You for helping me do good things. Help me not to get tired of doing them. Amen.

What's in My Heart

The Seed: He who searches our hearts knows the mind of the Spirit. *Romans 8:27*

Planting Time

What I say and what I do
Hold finger to lips, then spread arms wide.
May not be what I mean.
Shake head no.
God knows what's inside my heart,
Place hands over heart.
The thoughts not really seen.
Hold hands over eyes.

Jesus, make what's in my heart
Form cross with index fingers.
Match what I say and do.
Nod head yes.
Help me to have a heart like Yours—
Hold hands over heart.
Loving, kind, and true.
Hug each other.

Harvest Time: Tell your child about a time when you tried to look like you were doing something loving, but in your heart you were really thinking unkind thoughts. Explain that Jesus helps us with those times and fills us with His love so our actions match our thoughts. Cut hearts from paper. Give one to your child and say "Thank you for sharing Jesus' love" when you see her doing something kind this week.

My Prayer: Jesus, keep my thoughts and actions kind and true. Amen.

God's Family

The Seed: God ... accepts men from every nation who [love] Him. *Acts 10:34–35*

Planting Time

> You may be big and strong.
> > *Flex arm muscles.*
> You may be short or tall.
> > *Hold hand low, then high.*
> To God we're all the same—
> > *Point up.*
> He loves us all!
> > *Cross hands over heart.*
>
> You may come from far away
> > *Point far away.*
> Or not look like me at all.
> > *Point to self and shake head no.*
> To God we're all the same—
> > *Point up.*
> He loves us all!
> > *Cross hands over heart.*

Harvest Time: Cut pictures of many different children from newspapers, catalogs, or magazines. Help your child glue them to a sheet of paper to make a collage. Title your collage "God's Family," and hang it on the refrigerator or in your child's room. Teach your child the song "Jesus Loves the Little Children."

My Prayer: God, thank You for making such a big family. Thank You for loving us all. In Jesus' name. Amen.

Kind Words

The Seed: [You] have put on the new self. *Colossians 3:10*

Planting Time

>I can talk and talk
>>*Touch fingers and thumb to form a*
>>*talking mouth.*
>
>With this little mouth of mine.
>>*Point to lips.*
>
>God helps every word to be
>>*Point up.*
>
>Loving, wise, and kind.
>>*Cross hands over heart.*
>
>My lips and tongue can form the words
>>*Touch fingers and thumb to form a*
>>*talking mouth.*
>
>For this little mouth of mine,
>>*Point to lips.*
>
>But it is God who makes the words
>>*Point up.*
>
>Loving, wise, and kind.
>>*Cross hands over heart.*

Harvest Time: Thank your child for the loving and kind words he has used today. Explain that, by ourselves, we would never be able to keep from using unkind words. God fills us with love and faith and helps us to live as His children. Practice using kind words today.

My Prayer: God, I'm glad I'm Your child. Help me use kind words today. In Jesus' name. Amen.

Praising God

The Seed: Sing joyfully to the LORD. *Psalm 33:1*

Planting Time: *Clap or play rhythm instruments while you enjoy this poem with your child.*

> I will sing, sing, sing
> All the day long,
> Praises to God.
> He gives me my song.
>
> I will sing, sing, sing
> While I work, while I play,
> Praising my God
> For all of the day.
>
> I will sing, sing, sing
> All the day long,
> Praises to God.
> He gives me my song.

Harvest Time: Play pans, spoons, and lids to add rhythmic accompaniment to some of your child's favorite Jesus songs. Pick special songs to sing as prayers at mealtime and bedtime.

My Prayer: God, You are so great and so good! It makes me happy to sing songs and praise You. In Jesus' name. Amen.

Stand Up and Walk

The Seed: Silver or gold I do not have, but what I have I give you. *Acts 3:6*

Planting Time

>A man could not run or walk at all.
>>*Shake head no.*
>He had two crippled legs.
>>*Point to legs.*
>Friends carried him to the temple each day
>>*Hold arms out as if carrying someone.*
>And put him there to beg.
>>*Hold out cupped hands.*

>One day two men came walking by.
>>*Walk in place.*
>Their names were Peter and John.
>>*Count two fingers.*
>He asked them for some money, please,
>>*Hold out cupped hands.*
>Before they passed and were gone.
>>*Walk in place.*

>Peter saw those legs that could not walk
>>*Point to legs.*
>And spoke so very bold.
>>*Point to mouth.*
>He told the man to look at him,
>>*Point to eyes.*
>Said, "We have no silver or gold.
>>*Shake head no.*

"But something else I'll give to you,
Hold hands out.
By the power of Jesus Christ.
Form cross with index fingers.
You can walk and run today—
Nod head yes.
Stand up now, arise!"
Raise hands.

The man stood up on his two feet,
Stand up tall.
Not crippled in any way.
Shake head no.
He began to walk and jump around
Walk and jump in place.
And give to God the praise.
Fold hands.

Harvest Time: Read this story to your child from the Bible or a Bible storybook. Repeat the poem several times, letting your child play the parts of Peter and the crippled man. Help your child to understand that God healed the man. Peter was His helper. If your child, or someone your child knows, has a disability, discuss how God helps you and your child to deal with it.

My Prayer: God, thank You for my legs and my feet. In Jesus' name. Amen.

Okay

The Seed: Do everything without complaining or arguing. *Philippians 2:14*

Planting Time

> Just tell me what to do,
> > *Point to mouth.*
> I'll say okay.
> > *Touch index finger and thumb in an okay sign.*
> I'll never complain;
> > *Shake head no.*
> I'll do it right away.
> > *Nod head yes.*
>
> Just tell me what to do,
> > *Point to mouth.*
> I'll say okay.
> > *Touch index finger and thumb in an okay sign.*
> I'll never argue;
> > *Shake head no.*
> I'll do it right away.
> > *Nod head yes.*

Harvest Time: Cut a large star from a sheet of paper. Help your child use a marker to write "okay" in the center of the star. Explain that, as St. Paul continues in Philippians 2, when Jesus forgives us and helps us share His love, we shine like stars. Make a game of saying "okay" often today when you ask one another to do things.

My Prayer: Dear Jesus, thank You for making me shine like a star. Amen.

Jesus Lives

The Seed: I know that my Redeemer lives. *Job 19:25*

Planting Time

> I know that Jesus loves us.
> > *Cross hands over heart.*
> He died for everyone.
> > *Spread arms wide.*
> God sent Him to the cross for us,
> > *Form cross with index fingers.*
> His one and only Son.
> > *Hold up one finger.*
>
> God brought Him back
> > *Point up.*
> To life again—hurray!
> > *Cup hands around mouth and shout "Hurray!"*
> And now He lives in heaven,
> > *Point up.*
> Where we will live someday.
> > *Nod head yes.*

Harvest Time: It will be hard for your child to understand the sacrificial aspects of God's great love in sending His Son to die for us. Simply tell your child that Jesus loves us so much that He gave His life on the cross for us. When we see a cross, we think of how much Jesus loves us and how we will live with Him forever.

My Prayer: God, thank You for sending Jesus to live and die for me. Amen.

Sometimes I Forget

The Seed: Everyone who sins breaks the law. *1 John 3:4*

Planting Time

> I try to do my best
> To never break God's law.
> I try to mind my mom
> And never whine at all.
>
> But sometimes I forget
> What I'm supposed to do.
> Then I say "I'm sorry,"
> To Mom and to God too.

Harvest Time: Explain that we sin when we do what we want to do instead of what God wants us to do. Talk about a sin you have committed that your child will be able to understand. Demonstrate how you asked God for forgiveness. When your child does something wrong, teach her to say "I'm sorry" to the person she has hurt and to God. Then celebrate God's forgiveness in Jesus.

My Prayer: God, help me not to break Your law. Forgive me when I sin. In Jesus' name. Amen.

I Will Pray

The Seed: I want men everywhere to lift up holy hands in prayer. *1 Timothy 2:8*

Planting Time

> I pray for all the rulers
> Of my country, town, and state—
> From firefighter to president,
> They make our country great.
>
> I will obey the rules
> These leaders make for me.
> They keep me safe from danger
> And keep our country free.

Harvest Time: Help your child look for civic servants and leaders. Include these people in your daily prayers. Be a model for your child by respecting government leaders, even those with whom you disagree.

My Prayer: God, thank You for my leaders. Help them to be good leaders and make laws that please You. In Jesus' name. Amen.

God's Purpose

The Seed: I have [called] you by name; you are Mine.
Isaiah 43:1

Planting Time

> Everything,
> > *Spread arms wide.*
>
> Both large and small,
> > *Place hands far apart, then close*
> > *together.*
>
> God created it.
> > *Point up.*
>
> He made it all.
> > *Spread arms wide.*
>
> God has a purpose
> > *Point up.*
>
> For every thing,
> > *Spread arms wide.*
>
> From the creepy, crawly bug
> > *Crawl fingers up your arm.*
>
> To the bird that can sing.
> > *Flap arms like wings.*
>
> God has a purpose
> > *Point up.*
>
> For all that we see.
> > *Spread arms wide.*
>
> God has a purpose—
> > *Point up.*
>
> Even for me!
> > *Point to self.*

Harvest Time: Help your child make a list of his favorite things in God's creation. God asks us to take good care of His world. God sets us apart in His creation by calling us by name in our baptism and giving us the special purpose of telling the Good News about His Son, Jesus.

My Prayer: God, I love the world You made. And I love telling people about Jesus. Amen.

Let Them Come

The Seed: Let the little children come to Me.
Matthew 19:14

Planting Time

> "Let the children come to Me,"
> That's what Jesus said
> When the boys and girls
> By their moms and dads were led.
>
> They wanted to see Jesus,
> But His disciples told them, "No.
> He's too busy; not right now.
> You will have to go."
>
> Sadly, sadly the children turned,
> And then heard Jesus say,
> "Let the children come to Me;
> Let them come today."
>
> How they must have laughed with joy
> As they climbed on Jesus' knee.
> He held them close and said to them,
> "Let the children come to Me."

Harvest Time: Act out the poem together. Pretend you are Jesus and let your child climb onto your lap. Let her tell you what she would say to Jesus.

My Prayer: Jesus, I'm glad I can talk to You. Amen.

Following Jesus

The Seed: By this all men will know that you are My disciples, if you love one another. *John 13:35*

Planting Time

I like to follow Jesus;
Form cross with index fingers.
Where He leads, I go.
Walk in place.
Others know I belong to Him
Form cross with index fingers.
Because of the love I show.
Cross hands over heart.

I like to follow Jesus
Form cross with index fingers.
And do as He wants me to.
Nod head yes.
He helps me act in love
Cross hands over heart.
So others will follow too.
Walk in place.

Harvest Time: Play a game of "Follow the Leader" with your child. Explain that we follow Jesus by telling people about Him and sharing the love that He gives us. Help your child choose a loving thing to do for a friend or family member and help him to do it.

My Prayer: Jesus, help me share Your love so everyone will know that I follow You. Amen.

Oops! My Mistake

The Seed: Do not judge. *Matthew 7:1*

Planting Time

> I don't want to tattle
> > *Shake head no.*
> Or complain about you.
> > *Point to each other.*
> I'll just watch
> > *Shade eyes with hand.*
> The things that I do.
> > *Point to self.*
>
> We all do things wrong—
> > *Spread arms wide.*
> God calls it sin.
> > *Point up.*
> We tell God we're sorry,
> > *Fold hands and bow head.*
> And He forgives us again.
> > *Form cross with index fingers.*

Harvest Time: Talk about a time when you have sinned. Show your child how you repented and felt sure of God's forgiveness. Help your child say an "I'm sorry" prayer. Then celebrate God's forgiveness together.

My Prayer: God, please forgive my sins. In Jesus' name. Amen.

My Friend

The Seed: You are My friends if you do what I command. *John 15:14*

Planting Time

> I have a friend named Jesus.
> > *Form cross with index fingers.*
> He's number one with me.
> > *Hold up one finger.*
> He calls me "friend" and helps me
> > *Cross hands over heart.*
> And takes good care of me.
> > *Nod head yes.*
>
> I have a friend named Jesus.
> > *Form cross with index fingers.*
> He shows me what to do.
> > *Spread arms wide.*
> I'll tell you all about Him
> > *Point to mouth.*
> So you can love Him too.
> > *Cross hands over heart.*
>
> I have a friend named Jesus.
> > *Form cross with index fingers.*
> He even died for me.
> > *Continue to show cross.*
> And now He lives in heaven
> > *Point up.*
> And makes a place for me.
> > *Point to self.*

Harvest Time: Remind your child that we can learn about Jesus from God's Word and from pastors, teachers, and family members who teach us about Him. Let your child do something for her special friend Jesus—sing a song, draw a picture, help someone, learn a Bible verse.

My Prayer: Jesus, I'm glad You're my friend. Amen.

God Watches over Me

The Seed: He does not take His eyes off the righteous. *Job 36:7*

Planting Time

> God loves me and watches
> > *Cross hands over heart.*
>
> All that I do.
> > *Point to self.*
>
> He loves you and watches
> > *Cross hands over heart.*
>
> Over you too.
> > *Point to each other.*
>
> God sees through the night
> > *Rest cheek on hands.*
>
> And all the day long.
> > *Circle arms overhead to make sun.*
>
> He loves all His children—
> > *Spread arms wide.*
>
> To Him we belong.
> > *Point up.*

Harvest Time: Explain that God is always watching over your child to keep him safe. If he ever feels afraid, he can ask God to help him. He will help, even before he asks.

My Prayer: God, thank You for watching over me all the time. In Jesus' name. Amen.

On the Go

The Seed: I am with you always. *Matthew 28:20*

Planting Time

> High on a mountain
> > *Reach up high.*
> Or way, way down low,
> > *Touch the ground.*
> Jesus is with me
> > *Form cross with index fingers.*
> Wherever I go.
> > *Spread arms wide.*
>
> At night when I'm sleeping,
> > *Rest cheek on hands.*
> All day on the go,
> > *Run in place.*
> Jesus is with me
> > *Form cross with index fingers.*
> Wherever I go.
> > *Spread arms wide.*
>
> There's not a place I could be
> > *Shake head no.*
> That I wouldn't know
> > *Touch forehead.*
> That Jesus is with me
> > *Form cross with index fingers.*
> Wherever I go.
> > *Spread arms wide.*

Harvest Time: Pray as you fasten your seat belts in the car. Thank Jesus for going with you everywhere.

My Prayer: Jesus, I'm glad You're always with me. Amen.

Love Your Enemies

The Seed: Love your enemies. *Luke 6:27*

Planting Time: *The only unkindness your young child should experience for a while is being left out or having a toy taken by a sibling or friend. Explain that Jesus loved and forgave even the people who were unkind to Him. Let your child know it's okay to protect herself by saying "Please stop that," but that sharing the love and forgiveness of Jesus will strengthen a friendship.*

> If someone is mean
> Or unkind to you,
> Think of something kind
> That you can do.
>
> Forgive those
> Who are mean to you.
> Jesus did;
> He'll help you too.

Harvest Time: Talk with your child about someone who has been unkind to her recently. Pray together for that person, then make a treat or draw a picture for the person to show your forgiveness.

My Prayer: Jesus, help me to be kind and forgiving like You. Amen.

Heaven Is My Home

The Seed: We have … an eternal house in heaven.
2 Corinthians 5:1

Planting Time

> I have a home in heaven.
> It's the greatest place to be.
> I don't know what it looks like,
> But Jesus will be with me.
>
> I might see fields to run in.
> I might see trees to climb.
> I might find secret hiding places
> And warm weather all the time.
>
> I have a home in heaven.
> I will go to it some day.
> Jesus will be with me,
> And I will shout "Hurray!"

Harvest Time: Explain that one day Jesus will take us to heaven to live with Him. Heaven will be far better than birthday parties, Disneyland, or the most wonderful things that your child can imagine. In heaven we will be with Jesus. Help your child draw a picture of, or describe, what heaven might be like.

My Prayer: Jesus, thank You for my home in heaven. It will be wonderful to live with You. Amen.

I Believe

The Seed: Whoever believes in the Son has eternal life. *John 3:36*

Planting Time

> I believe in Jesus.
> > *Form cross with index fingers.*
> Yes, I really do!
> > *Nod head yes.*
> I'll live with Him in heaven
> > *Point up.*
> When my life on earth is through.
> > *Hug self.*
>
> I believe in Jesus.
> > *Form cross with index fingers.*
> Yes, I really do!
> > *Nod head yes.*
> I'll live with Him forever
> > *Spread arms wide.*
> When my life on earth is through.
> > *Hug self.*

Harvest Time: The concept of having faith, or believing, will be difficult for your child. Explain that it means trusting Jesus to take care of us and knowing He loves us so much that He gave His life for us. Sing some of your favorite songs about Jesus. Serve treats on special dishes to celebrate being able to live forever with Jesus.

My Prayer: Jesus, I'm glad I believe in You. Amen.